Smart Marketing
For Local Businesses

POPULAR ARTICLES BY TRUDY MURPHY

- ✓ Increase sales immediately with this one small change
- ✓ The 7 Deadly Business Sins
- ✓ Startup Advice: Two Ways Your Support Network Fails You
- ✓ 5 Steps to 6 Figures & Beyond
- ✓ Stand Out or Stand Down
- ✓ Why Loyalty Programs Work & How You Can Use Them To Compete With The Big Boys
- ✓ How to Know What Your Customers Think Before They Yelp
- ✓ How to Sell More Without Discounting or Marketing
- ✓ Amazon Is Slowly Killing Retailers

Available at www.trudymurphy.com

Smart Marketing
For Local Businesses

A practical guide for driving customers to your door, not fans to a page.

Trudy Murphy

Copyright © 2013 by Trudy Murphy

All Rights Reserved. No part of this publication may be reproduced, distributed or transmitted in any form or by any means, including scanning, photocopying, or otherwise without prior written permission of the copyright holder, except for use as brief quotations embodied in critical reviews and certain other noncommercial uses as permitted by copyright law. Contact the publisher to request permission.

Published by Brio Risk Management Inc.
Toronto, Canada
www.brioriskmanagement.com

1st Edition, 1st Printing, April 2013
2nd Edition, 2nd Printing, April 2016
ISBN-13: 978-1483905143
ISBN-10: 1483905144

DEDICATION

This book is dedicated to every entrepreneur.

Never give up your big, audacious dreams.

CONTENTS

PART ONE - MINDSET	**11**
EVEN ACCOUNTANTS NEED MARKETING	13
SET YOURSELF UP FOR SUCCESS	16
PART TWO – MARKETING STEMS FROM WITHIN	**19**
A QUICK INTERNAL CHECK	21
PRICING	25
KEY TAKEAWAYS	34
PART THREE – THE SMART MARKETING PLAN	**35**
STEP 1: CREATE THE OFFER	37
STEP 2: DEFINE & SELECT THE MARKETING CAMPAIGNS	40
STEP 3: MONITOR, RECORD & EVALUATE RESULTS	43
PART FOUR – THE INTERNET & SOCIAL MEDIA	**45**
WEBSITES AND EMAIL LISTS	47
SEARCH ENGINE OPTIMIZATION	50
SOCIAL MEDIA IS OPTIONAL FOR LOCAL BUSINESSES	54
A WORD OF CAUTION ON HIRING "EXPERTS"	57
KEY TAKEAWAYS	59
PART FIVE – SMART MARKETING IDEAS	**61**
SPARKING CREATIVITY	63
IDEA #1 - TARGET YOUR IDEAL CLIENTS	65
IDEA #2 - NETWORK	66
IDEA #3 - GET CREATIVE WITH BUSINESS CARDS	71
IDEA #4 - SPEAK AT EVENTS	72

IDEA #5 - HOST EVENTS	74
IDEA #6 - WRITE GUEST POSTS	77
IDEA #7 - CREATE STRATEGIC PARTNERSHIPS	78
IDEA #8 - ATTEND CHARITY EVENTS	80
IDEA #9 - RENT YOUR SPACE	83
IDEA #10 - BE NEWSWORTHY & CREATE A MEDIA KIT	86
IDEA #11 - BE "THE BEST" IN YOUR CITY	88
IDEA #12 - EXHIBIT AT TRADE SHOWS	91
IDEA #13 - CREATE PROMOTIONAL OFFERS	94
IDEA #14 - CONSTANTLY UP-SELL	96
IDEA #15 - ADVERTISE	97
IDEA #16 - LOYALTY AND REFERRAL PROGRAMS	98
KEY TAKEAWAYS	100
PART SIX – THE MARKETING HIERARCHY OF SUCCESS	**103**
HOW TO MARKET YOUR BUSINESS LIKE A PRO	105
PART SEVEN – ACTION CREATES INSPIRATION	**113**
5 TIPS FOR BEING A KICK BUTT MARKETER!	115
FINALIZE YOUR SMART MARKETING PLAN & EXECUTE	119
KEY TAKEAWAYS	120
COMMIT TO YOUR GOALS	**121**
ABOUT THE AUTHOR	**123**

PART ONE - MINDSET

"I believe life is constantly testing us for our level of commitment and life's greatest rewards are reserved for those who demonstrate a never-ending commitment to act until they achieve. This level of resolve can move mountains, but it must be constant and consistent. As simplistic as this may sound, it is still the common denominator separating those who live their dreams from those who live in regret."

- Tony Robbins

PART ONE - MINDSET

Even Accountants Need Marketing

Have you ever looked back at a time in your life and thought, *"Damn, if only I knew then what I know now?"* I'm sure you have; we all have. Well, this book is a product of one of those moments for me. This book is my gift to you, so hopefully you can avoid THAT moment in some way.

You may be reading this book without knowing anything at all about me, so let me give you my brief background. I'm an accountant. Yes, I know what you're thinking, *"Why the hell are YOU writing a book about marketing?"* Because, whilst I originally trained as an accountant, my career has taken me on a path where I've owned two local businesses and operated as an independent business consultant to some of the world's largest multinational corporations.

I spent years gaining technical certifications in accounting and finance, but when it came to marketing my local businesses, I had to start from scratch. I spent countless hours researching marketing strategies, testing theories and following the advice of "experts" who had never actually owned a local business. Throughout this book I'll candidly share with you both my successes and mistakes when launching and growing my 3 local businesses (an organic hair salon and day spa; a social event company; and a consulting services firm).

What I've realized during my journey is that marketing doesn't need to be difficult. But for many entrepreneurs, marketing can feel overwhelming when it's not your forte. There is so much information out there it's difficult to know which marketing strategies will deliver the greatest results on a limited budget. So a common path for business owners is to bounce from tactic to tactic, trying anything, but not sticking to any sort of plan or strategy. Along the way they spend countless dollars on untracked campaigns that leave them clueless as to what works and what doesn't.

On the flip side are the hundreds of entrepreneurs I meet every year who read and learn and attend conferences, but never actually launch anything. These entrepreneurs spend time and money generating ideas and contemplating next steps, while missing the most important lesson of all; action creates inspiration.

In understanding that entrepreneurs are generally short on time, cash and focus, I've intentionally made this book short in length but filled with actionable ideas for a shoestring budget. In this book, you will not find long-winded stories that labour on points or prescriptive methods for success. What you will find is a succinct and practical guide that's intended to help you develop a marketing plan, provoke fresh ideas and elicit your resourcefulness. In the following pages, I'll simplify the world of marketing for you based on real experience and expel some of the myths around social media. I guarantee the "experts" won't like what I have to say on that topic.

Set Yourself Up For Success

In this book I'll share with you a bunch of ideas for marketing your local business. Some of them will work for you and some of them won't. But the fact is, none of them will work if you don't create a plan to implement anything. So before we start, let's create an outline for an extremely simple marketing plan that we'll continue to develop throughout the book. When you reach the end of this book you will have an effective and actionable marketing strategy that you can start implementing today.

Let's do this right now.

Grab a piece of paper and a pen or open a word document and create a table with 6 columns and 16 rows. Use the first row to label each column. Write the word "Questions" at the top of the first column and number the other columns 1 to 5.

If you would prefer to download the Smart Marketing Plan and free training, simply visit: **www.smartmarketingforlocalbusinesses.com/the-plan**

PART ONE - MINDSET

In the first column of the Smart Marketing Plan, type the following questions into the first 5 rows.

1. Who are my ideal customers?

2. Where are they located?

3. What pain are they experiencing or what need do they have?

4. What solutions or offers would I like to share with them?

5. Why will they care? What are the benefits of my solution/offer that solve my customer's problem?

Now that you have the starting framework of your Smart Marketing Plan, set it aside for now and continue reading. We'll return to it and answer these questions and more soon.

PART TWO – MARKETING STEMS FROM WITHIN

"A brand is something you are portraying every single second of every single day. So you are portraying that brand when you walk down the street, when you go to a party, when you stand in line at Tim Horton's ... If you're trying to distinguish yourself as a high quality brand and you're handing out cards with a hotmail address, you're going to have to change that as it doesn't go along with the brand ... or if I go to your website and certain buttons don't work, then your brand is being shot. Everything you do is an opportunity to solidify your brand."

- Stuart Knight

─── PART TWO – MARKETING STEMS FROM WITHIN ───

A Quick Internal Check

Let's do a quick internal check of your business to see if there are any areas for improvement in the way you currently attract and retain customers. Take a look around your store, at yourself, your website and honestly answer the following questions:

- Is your company's value proposition[1] clear, concise and convincing?

- Does your brand reflect your company's value proposition?

- Does your marketing material (business cards, promotional items, website etc.) have a consistent look that represents your brand?

- Do you walk your talk? Are you portraying your brand every second of every single day?

- Are you building credibility, earning trust and adding value every day?

---

[1] A company's value proposition is a clear and concise statement

- Does your receptionist answer the phone and greet every customer with a smile and welcoming demeanor?

- Are the store window displays and signage interesting and appealing? Do they attract the attention of passers-by and make them want to come in?

- Does the store layout make sense such that customers and staff can easily move through the store? Can they easily find, try and buy products?

- Are product displays clean and well laid out? Do you change displays regularly to keep loyal customers interested and to promote products of the month or specials?

- Does the counter area make it easy for the cashier to up-sell items and quickly assist customers to cash-out?

- Do all of your staff have a basic knowledge of all products and services offered so they can speak with confidence to up-sell or answer questions about an offering that is not their main specialty?

PART TWO – MARKETING STEMS FROM WITHIN

- Does your cashier ask every customer if they enjoyed their experience?

- During check-out, does your cashier ask every customer if they would like to book their next appointment?

- Does every service and product you offer, meet or exceed your customer's expectations?

- Are you WOWING your customers every time you interact with them?

- Are you thanking your customers for their loyalty?

- Are you talking to your customers regularly, soliciting feedback and responding?

- Are you using poor reviews to engage with your customers and improve your offerings?

- Do you have a process to solicit feedback from staff on a regular basis?

- What needs to be improved, changed, added or removed from your business today?

Take a moment to write out your answers. If you don't know the answer to any of these questions, ask your staff or customers, they will know.

When I work with entrepreneurs to transform their business, one of my first action steps is to interview their staff. Ninety nine percent of the time employees know where the weak points are in the business and which customer needs the company is failing to meet. Are you giving your staff the opportunity to contribute ideas? Are you listening?

Once you've talked to your staff, take a look at your customer reviews. If you don't have a process to solicit and respond to customer feedback, you're missing vital opportunities to grow your business and protect your reputation. Ensure your customers have a safe way to give feedback before they leave your store and that staff are trained to record responses and handle complaints immediately. If you're not asking customers for feedback, they will share it online with everyone, regardless of whether you want to hear it or not.

Are there changes you've been meaning to make for a while but haven't gotten around to it yet? Write your action list now and commit to a deadline for implementing change.

Pricing

You'll notice in the previous section I did not mention pricing. This is because it is such an important topic I wanted to address it separately.

I've heard many business owners complain over the years that business is tough because people aren't willing to pay the price that their product or service is worth. Let me be brutally honest with you here, that statement is complete bollocks! If you have a quality product or service that meets a customer's need and solves their problem, there will always be people willing to buy it at the price it is worth. The real problem is that you are struggling in one or more of the following three critical areas of business.

1. Industry Trends and Competition

Every industry has different characteristics that determine its structure; the way in which market players operate; and the degree of power that buyers and sellers exude in the marketplace. The potential to profit in an industry is ultimately determined by, what Michael Porter[2] defined as the five competitive market

---

[2] Porter, M.E. (1979) *How Competitive Forces Shape Strategy*, *Harvard Business Review*, March/April 1979.

forces.

In Porter's *"Five Forces Analysis"* he identified the characteristics that determine how profitable a business can be in any industry. His analysis shows that low margin industries are usually highly competitive with many sellers able to easily enter the market and where buyers can easily switch between substitute products and services due to low levels of differentiation.

Consider these concepts in relation to your own business by answering the following questions:

- When you started your business, did you do an industry analysis?

- Do you stay up to date with current trends and changes?

- Do you know where your business is positioned in your industry and who your closest competitors are?

- Do you know how much your competition charges for services or products and whether you are at the high, middle or low end of your industry?

When you clearly understand and stay up to date with the environment in which your company operates, you can formulate an effective strategy to position it for success.

PART TWO – MARKETING STEMS FROM WITHIN

Let me demonstrate by discussing the spa industry. It is a highly competitive market with many players that can easily enter and set up shop. There is the low end, cheap mani/pedi/waxing spas and the very high end, resort style luxury spas that clients happily travel to for a treat. Then there is a huge range of middle of the road spas that offer the same type of services, at similar price points.

When making a purchasing decision, clients in the spa industry evaluate the following factors:

- Price

- Customer Service

- Product Quality

- Location

- Atmosphere

- Cleanliness

Every customer will place a different level of value on each of these factors when making their buying decision.

Your job as a business owner is to identify the factors each customer segment cares about and then decide which group of customers you want to attract. By placing emphasis on the same factors they value most when making their buying decisions, you have the formula for attracting the clients you want. I'll explain more below.

2. Positioning

If people are telling you they can't afford your services, ask yourself "What type of customer am I attracting?"

I once asked this of a client who was frustrated that potential customers could not afford his services. When we looked at the market segment that was rejecting his offer based on price, that group mainly consisted of unemployed people. Well, of course they can't afford high end services, but they did have a need for a solution so we created a new program specifically for them at a lower price point.

Once you have identified the type of customer that's walking away based on price, you have one of two options available to you:

1. Decide they are not your target audience anyway and don't give it anymore thought.
2. Create a new lower priced offer that solves their problem.

Now, the two options above are based on the assumption that your business is doing just fine without these customers. But, if your business is struggling because your total sales conversion rate is very low, you have a positioning and/or packaging problem that needs to be addressed immediately.

Communication of important differences between your business and your competitors is the basis for a successful positioning strategy. Let's continue with the spa industry example.

I owned a local neighborhood hair salon and day spa in downtown Toronto. The local area residents were generally professionals (approx. 25-45 years old) who enjoyed eating out, shopping and lived in a trendy part of town. The street where the spa was located consisted of many newly opened and very busy restaurants and bars with meals ranging in price from $20 - $40 per plate. New apartment buildings were under construction in the area and at the time we opened there were no other salons or spas. This analysis of the area helped us determine the type and range of customers that lived within, or were willing to travel to, our neighborhood.

So here's how we positioned the spa. We wanted to attract the professional who was not concerned about price provided they received outstanding customer service, high quality products and enjoyed a comfortable experience in a very clean, but not necessarily luxurious, environment. We looked at competitive spas in the city that targeted the same clientele in order to define our service list and pricing. To differentiate ourselves from the competition, we sourced organic products to use in services and to retail.

PART TWO – MARKETING STEMS FROM WITHIN

The use of organic products had three advantages:

1. It provided differentiation;

2. It instantly created an expectation of higher pricing in the minds of customers (the words "certified organic", regardless of product, does this to people); and

3. It enabled us to not only market to the local neighborhood residents, but to attract a type of customer that was willing to travel to buy services or products that met their lifestyle standards (a green and eco-friendly buying criteria).

Then we created the tagline that succinctly communicated our market positioning "Your one-stop-shop for organic pampering".

Take a moment to consider the following questions:

- What is your company's current market position? Is it where you would like it to be in your industry?

- How are you communicating your desired market position to your customers?

- If you provide services, how are you showing the world your knowledge and expertise to establish your market position?

- Are you viewed as an expert in your field, leader in your industry or the "go-to-place" in your neighborhood?

- Do you have client testimonials that support your market position?

3. Packaging

Now that you know the characteristics and values of your target audience, you must package your business and offers in a way that appeals to that audience, while simultaneously ensuring everything is congruent with the market position you're communicating. You must also ensure that your offers match the level of trust you have developed with your customer. It's always a good idea to create a lower priced introductory offer that gets your foot in the door with the client. Then, as you build trust by consistently delivering value, you can pitch higher priced and longer term offers.

With a bricks and mortar store, like the spa we've been discussing, take a walk through and follow the steps your customers take through your store. Sit where they would sit; stand where they would stand. What can they see? How does it feel? How does it sound? If you were a customer, what would elevate your experience from good to great?

Now think about your customer offers, how can you improve the packaging to up the WOW factor? How does your market positioning and packaging build your brand? Does the packaging match the customer's expectation given their level of trust and the price being charged?

Key Takeaways

- ✓ The competitive forces in your specific industry, ultimately determine profitability and therefore pricing.

- ✓ Pricing is a function of market positioning and packaging.

- ✓ Market positioning and packaging is your brand and they must always be congruent.

- ✓ Make sure everything about your business is building your brand, not shooting it down.

- ✓ Check your ego at the door and take a good honest look around you. Listen, see things as they are and take corrective action.

- ✓ Constantly ask for feedback from all stakeholders and do something with it.

- ✓ WOW your customers and say thank you.

PART THREE – THE SMART MARKETING PLAN

"A goal without a plan is just a wish."

- Antoine de Saint-Exupéry

PART THREE – THE SMART MARKETING PLAN

Step 1: Create The Offer

Take a moment to think about what you've read so far and the questions posed. Give yourself the luxury of time to breathe and reflect on how you've been operating your business to date and how you would like it to be in the future. Since you're reading this book, I know you're looking for impactful change. So let's capture your thoughts in a structured and actionable way.

Take out the Smart Marketing Plan we created earlier in part one of this book or visit **www.smartmarketingforlocalbusinesses.com/the-plan** to download your free copy.

Using the information you've just read, lets write answers to questions 1 through 5 in your marketing plan.

1. *Who are my ideal customers?* When identifying your ideal customers in question 1, include as much information about them and their lifestyle as possible. The more detail you include about your ideal customer's profile now, the easier you will find it to create effective marketing strategies that target your audience. You will likely have more than one ideal customer profile, therefore write

each customer profile into the separate columns. For example, the high-level answers to question 1 for a Beauty Spa might look like this:

Column 1: "Brides & bridal parties"

Column 2: "Group events e.g. bachelorette parties, baby showers"

Column 3: "Special event attendees e.g. prom, film festival parties"

Column 4: "Professional women aged 25-50"

Column 5: "People living an organic, eco-friendly lifestyle"

2. ***Where are they located?*** Under each customer profile, write where they are located. This question has been purposefully separated out, as location targeting is critical to creating effective marketing campaigns for local businesses.

3. ***What pain are they experiencing or what need do they have?*** Describe the pain or problem each ideal customer is experiencing[3]. Try to use the wording your ideal customers would use to describe their problem. Using your customer's

---

[3] If a customer profile has more than one problem, add another column, repeat that customer profile at the top and write unique answers to each question.

words will help you to connect with them when writing copy for your marketing material. I'll talk more about writing copy later in this book.

4. *What solutions or offers would I like to share with them?* For each problem you've identified, describe the solution(s) you will provide.

5. *Why will they care? What are the benefits of my offer that solves my customer's problem?* Describe the benefits of your solutions. Try to match a benefit to every problem stated at 3 above. For example, when marketing spa services to brides, we identified that brides were afraid they wouldn't receive the services promised and that they would be surprised with overcharging on their wedding day. Our solution was to document everything in a contract for the bride and finalize all payments including gratuities prior to the wedding. These benefits might be described as follows:

> *We clearly communicate all details and pricing in advance through written contracts so a bride never has to worry about overcharging, miscommunication or any other upsetting surprise on her big day.*

Step 2: Define & Select The Marketing Campaigns

Now that we've identified our ideal customers, their problems and our offers, it's time to create the framework for step 2 of your Smart Marketing Plan. Type the following questions into column 1, rows 6-10 of your plan. Don't worry about writing answers at this point, we'll come back to this later.

6. *What is the optimal platform[4] to engage with my customers and make this offer?* The following two chapters of this book are dedicated to discussing a variety of marketing ideas you can use to attract customers to your local business. As you read each idea, quickly write it into your plan at question 6 in the appropriate column(s). To start with, don't spend too much time thinking about how you would implement the idea, just follow a brainstorming technique and jot down the ideas you like and want to try. When you reach the end of the book, you'll have the high-level outline of your Smart Marketing Plan.

---

[4] A "platform" is the place where you will meet and connect with your customers e.g. twitter, trade shows, e-newsletters.

PART THREE – THE SMART MARKETING PLAN

7. *How will I implement this campaign? What is my capacity to execute and support this marketing campaign (budget, time, resources, ability and effort)?* Once you've finished reading and brainstorming ideas, review your plan and write detailed answers to questions 6 through 9. You'll find that as you flesh out these details, it will become clear which ideas you'll be able to implement quickly and which ones will be difficult or take more time.

8. *How will I track the return on investment[5] (ROI)? How will I know if this campaign has been successful?* ROI is a performance indicator that is most useful when it is quantified and used in the decision making process of evaluating results and comparing the relative success of multiple campaigns. Many people (including paid consultants) will state that the benefit of a marketing campaign is brand awareness, which is intangible and can't be quantified. However, unless your business is already wildly profitable and you have money to burn, I would urge you to focus on campaigns that have a quantifiable ROI so you can clearly evaluate the results of your campaigns and your valuable time and resources.

---

[5] The return on investment (ROI) is the benefit received from the marketing campaign minus the total cost of execution.

9. *What other products, services or bonuses can I provide as an upsell or gift with this offer?* I'll discuss upselling a number of times throughout the rest of the book. For now, I'd like you to know that one of the simplest and fastest ways to increase sales is to simply sell more to your existing customers during the sales process.

10. *Will I use this strategy? (Yes/No) If yes, when? If no, why not?* Complete this question to document which ideas you will and won't move forward with and set deadlines for yourself.

In answering question 10, make sure you prioritize the campaigns you've decided to move forward with by setting realistic and achievable timelines. A good way to prioritize campaigns is either in order based on ease of implementation or on the expected ROI from highest to lowest return.

As entrepreneurs, our brains constantly flood with ideas on how we can push our business forward. It's important to allow ideas to flow then realistically evaluate their merits and your available resources to execute successfully amidst your competing priorities. Not every idea should be pursued today.

Step 3: Monitor, Record & Evaluate Results

The first two steps in the Smart Marketing Plan are to prepare you to effectively and strategically execute your marketing campaigns. Step 3 (this step) takes place during and after the implementation of each campaign. Take a moment now to bookmark this page so you can easily return to it at any time.

Write the following questions into column 1, rows 11-15 of your plan.

11. *Describe how the marketing campaign was executed (this may be the same or different to the way you envisioned the details initially at 7 above).* Complete this question during or soon after the end of the campaign while the details are fresh in your memory. Include as much detail as possible such as supplier contact details, cost breakdown, resources utilized etc. This information will help you to efficiently repeat the campaign in the future if desired and assist with the evaluation of results.

12. *What lessons did you learn? What worked? What would you change next time?* Taking the time to review and capture lessons learned is critical to the efficient execution of future campaigns and to the successful evolution of your business. Not to mention, it will save you money in the long run and I know every business owner likes that.

13. *Overall, was the campaign successful? Record your return on investment and results of any other performance indicators or unexpected outcomes.* Revisit your answers to question 8 above where you described how you will determine the success of the campaign. For each performance indicator listed at question 8, write the corresponding result here. The campaign may have yielded different results to the ones you originally expected, include as much detail about the results as you can.

14. *Will you use this strategy again? Yes / No* Based on the results you captured at 13, will you repeat this campaign?

15. *If yes, when? Commit to a deadline. If no, why not?* Complete this question to document which ideas you will and won't repeat and set deadlines for yourself. Use your answer to this question as the starting point for creating your Smart Marketing Plan in the following year.

PART FOUR – THE INTERNET & SOCIAL MEDIA

"It's much easier to double your business by doubling your conversion rate than by doubling your traffic."

- Jeff Eisenberg

Websites and Email Lists

I would like to address the subject of online marketing at the outset of this chapter so we can move on to more direct marketing ideas for your local business.

Firstly, if you don't have a website, it's time to create one. People rely on the internet for finding information, products and services they need. You must be there for them or they'll be calling your competitors instead.

Your website should be optimized to work for you as an extension of your business, to build opt-in email lists, sell products and promotions (if applicable) and ultimately persuade visitors to trust and buy from you. I could write a whole book just on this subject alone, but this book is not about internet marketing so I don't intend to go into a lot of detail here.

Instead, I will list the very basic elements I believe your website should include:

1. A clear description of your business and the products and services you provide. When writing copy for your website, be sure to refer back to the ideal customer profiles created in response to questions 1 to 5 of your Smart Marketing Plan. Marketing copy often flows more easily when we

can imagine the type of customer we want the website to attract.

2. A reason and place for visitors to enter their email contact details. Give people a reason to opt-in to your email list such as, "Get a free quote", "Download this free e-book", "View this free training video" etc. Your email list is one of the most valuable assets in your business. Nurture it wisely and it will help you grow exponentially.

3. The backend of each web page should be complete with page titles, descriptions and meta tags. These data elements tell search engines what your website is about and therefore, will help customers find you in relevant search results. When targeting customers in your local geographic area, be sure to include your location in website meta tags.

4. Website content should include specific, targeted keywords that potential customers would type into search engines to find your products or services.

5. Verify your site with each search engine and ensure your business is listed with Google. This is especially important for local businesses as listing with Google will add your company information to Google Maps and help to increase your website ranking in search results.

PART FOUR – THE INTERNET & SOCIAL MEDIA

The above list is an extremely basic checklist to get you started if you're new to website creation. On the next few pages I'll provide some more ideas for increasing traffic to your website, but if the above is all you have time for when launching your business, that's ok for now.

Search Engine Optimization

In writing a book about marketing, I would be remiss if I didn't discuss online marketing and search engine optimization ("SEO"). However, there are many great books available that are solely dedicated to this massive subject, so I will not linger here for long. Instead, I'll provide you with the following list of tactics that I've personally used to rank my website higher in search results, to increase traffic to my website and build my email list.

The following list is by no means exhaustive and more detailed "how to" information on each tactic can be easily found through an internet search.

1. Hire an SEO specialist to make sure your website is optimized and your efforts are targeting appropriate keywords.

2. If you sell online products, list your business in online shopping malls.

3. Submit your website link and business description to free online business directories.

4. Create "How To" videos related to your area of expertise. Post them to video sites such as youtube.com including a link back to your

PART FOUR – THE INTERNET & SOCIAL MEDIA

website in the video description field.

5. Write a blog with great content and promote each post on your social media sites and other online platforms.

6. Submit articles as guest posts on other blog and news sites including a short bio and link back to your website.

7. Ping your website every time you add new content.

8. Create content specific micro-sites on free blogger websites such as Tumblr, Wordpress and Squidoo.

9. Participate in forums and communities by answering questions and sharing your knowledge. The key to successfully executing this strategy is to be genuinely helpful and absolutely resist any temptation to blatantly promote your business.

10. Provide a free gift on your social media sites to drive traffic to your website and increase email list opt-ins.

11. Post your free stuff on sites that specialize in promoting free stuff. For example, if you're promoting a limited time free offer on your kindle book, there are many sites that specialize

in promoting free kindle book offers to their email list.

12. Post your promo discounts or coupons on sites that specialize in identifying discounts for their visitors.

13. Make sure your email signature includes your contact details, a link to your website and an eye grabbing element such as a special offer, interesting quote, promotion of testimonials or media coverage on your business.

14. Submit press releases to free sites to announce big events such as a launch party, new product release or limited time promotion.

15. Use free link exchanges with topic relevant websites.

16. Google your top competitors, then submit your business data to every site where they are listed.

17. Share great content created by other people (make sure you provide a unique comment as to why you are sharing it). There are online tools that identify the most shared social media content by topic that can help to reduce the time spent on this marketing activity. Run an internet search for "Find Shareable Content" to view lists of available tools.

18. Post ads for events and promos on craigslist and other free classifieds sites.

19. Interview experts on topics relevant to your field and target audience. Consider using a social video platform to live stream the interview to attract new visitors to your website.

20. Write a book or create an audio product and self-publish it via online bookstores such as Amazon or Smash Words or audio sites such as Audible.

Some form of search engine optimization should be an ongoing part of your marketing activities. To maximize revenue, it's imperative that as many people can find you as possible and search engine optimization helps with that.

If content creation and online marketing is an integral part of your marketing plan, make sure you setup your process to maximize your efforts. In other words, if you create a video, use the audio to create a podcast, transcribe the video into text for a blog post then compile your blog posts into a book. Leverage your content creation efforts by distributing it through every medium possible. These days, people have their favorite ways to consume content so you need to use every media format available in order to reach as many people as possible.

Social Media Is Optional For Local Businesses

Social media has enabled businesses to communicate publicly on a global scale for free. But for the most part, I believe, it's confused and burdened many business owners. In my opinion, the local store owner, who's happy selling to neighborhood residents and the freelancer who works on contract with local companies, doesn't need social media to the extent the experts would like you to believe.

The first question you need to ask yourself is: how big does my geographic reach need to be? This will determine how much of your effort should be focused on online marketing and social media. As your need to reach a larger geographic region in order to generate revenue, increases, so too does your need to expand your online presence. Therefore, your online and offline marketing efforts should be aligned with your projected ratio of online and offline sales revenue.

However, here is the catch. Every business should establish their presence on every social media platform where their customers might comment, share, like, thumbs up, join events, check-in, etc. If they are going to take any of these actions, you want them to do it on your "official" platform. If you don't create the platform, loyal fans will, and then you'll lose control over the logo, photos, descriptions etc. that people will post to represent your business. And that is bad.

So, regardless of whether you intend to post social media content, it is important to create the official social media platforms for your business. This allows customers to find and connect with your business on any platform where they feel comfortable.

Social media should not be hard work. You need to make it work for you, not the other way around. Here are a few ideas on how to do this.

Use tools to:

- Be notified when people talk about you outside your platforms. For example, set up Google Alerts so you're notified by email whenever Google detects new content on the web that includes your business name.

- Be notified by email from LinkedIn and other job sites about potential contracts if you're a freelancer. Make sure your profile is complete and the description is keyword optimized so potential clients can find you in a search.

- Help people find you. Post videos to youtube, and other sites and submit articles to blog sites, if that's a strategy you want to use, but make sure every post includes a call to action that drives visitors to your website.

- Minimize the time you spend on social media. Tools such as Hootsuite enable you to send out status posts and chat with customers across all platforms without logging in to the individual websites.

If you're using social media to promote your business but you're not getting likes to your page or followers on your twitter account, don't let it stress you out. If you are inconsistent or just plain terrible at writing compelling status updates and blog posts, use a different marketing tactic that works for you, there's plenty out there.

Building a community with social media does not necessarily increase your customer base. As a local business it's critical that you know how you will convert community into customers. Investing time or money into building a community that doesn't buy from you is futile. If you don't enjoy online marketing, then focus on more direct customer acquisition strategies that drive customers to your door. Your time and energy are finite so choose your activities wisely.

A Word of Caution on Hiring "Experts"

Let me tell you a story about an experience I had with a virtual SEO expert. After reading Tim Ferriss's thought-provoking book, *"The 4-Hour Work Week"*, I was struck by the idea of hiring a virtual assistant to help rank one of my websites on the first page of Google. I shopped around and checked out a few different companies and eventually hired an SEO assistant in India to work 4 hours every day for 2 months.

The goal was to list my website on the first page of Google for specific keywords and to improve my company's social media presence with regular status updates and adding friends/followers to my platforms. The company I hired assured me they had a team of content creators who were fluent in English that would write original articles and status posts for my review prior to being released on the Internet.

The project turned out to be a slight nightmare when I reviewed the articles and found most of them contained plagiarized text taken directly from my competitor's websites. Fortunately, I picked up on it and killed the articles before they were distributed across the web.

The moral of this story is that there are no shortcuts.

Your online presence across all platforms should reflect the conversation you want to have with your customers. You must take direct responsibility for the content that generates the conversation because it's the only element that you can control online.

If you do outsource work to a PR, SEO, marketing agency or the like, make sure you have systems in place to monitor the work and put a stop to any sub-par content before it's released. In today's fast moving, information driven, customer centric world, it only takes one bad or offensive post to cause a large percentage of your audience to hide or unsubscribe from you. Not to mention the potential ongoing damage to your reputation if that content goes viral.

If you aren't consistently creating great online content, keeping up with tech changes and doing social media well, leave it to your loyal fans to generate your social presence. You're better off focusing your energy on direct local marketing strategies that drive customers to your door, not fans to a page. The rest of this book is dedicated to discussing those strategies.

So, pull out your Smart Marketing Plan and let's get started on brainstorming marketing ideas to complete question 6 of your plan.

PART FOUR – THE INTERNET & SOCIAL MEDIA

Key Takeaways

- ✓ You must have a website that is an extension of your brand if you're to be taken seriously as a competitive business in today's marketplace.

- ✓ Speak directly with your customers by email. Constantly look for ways to build and nurture your email opt-in list. Customer data is a business asset.

- ✓ Online and social media marketing are optional for local businesses that don't have eCommerce revenue. However, if you have a content planning and conversion strategy, it can be worth the investment if you can do it well. If not, don't worry about it.

- ✓ Always own your brand wherever people are talking about your business, regardless of whether you're generating the conversation or not.

- ✓ Community does not equal customers. If you're spending time building a community with social media, make sure you have a conversion strategy.

- ✓ Whenever you outsource work or employ someone, you still need to be involved to a degree and provide direction and strategy. The work doesn't just magically shift off your plate and happen without you.

- ✓ Always review and vet the content that's released online by your business. This is the only part of online marketing and social media that you can control.

PART FIVE – SMART MARKETING IDEAS

"Excellence is never an accident. It is always the result of high intention, sincere effort, and intelligent execution; it represents the wise choice of many alternatives - choice, not chance, determines your destiny."

- Aristotle

PART FIVE – SMART MARKETING IDEAS

Sparking Creativity

It just takes a small interaction to spark a perfectly creative idea that can propel your business forward. One night I was talking to a local restaurant owner who was explaining how his new greeter on the door was also working during the day to build partnerships between his restaurant and the local hotels. That conversation sparked a partnership idea that became extremely profitable for my own business. You'll find the details later in this chapter in the section "Creating Strategic Partnerships".

The interaction with the restaurant owner showed me that ideas come from the most unlikely sources and often when you least expect it. I'd like to encourage you to read each of the following ideas in this chapter and as you finish each one, ask yourself, "How can this work for me?"

At first glance of the idea titles that follow, you might initially decide that an idea such as tradeshows, aren't something you want to do. In making that decision you may be tempted to skip reading the content. I implore you to resist skipping through. Take the time to digest the content and see if there is a way that you can take the concept presented and make it your own.

In the immortal words of Bruce Springsteen *"You can start a fire without a spark"*[6]. Now, if you have *"Dancing in the Dark"* stuck in your head, you're welcome. Use it as a fun reminder to pause and reflect on each of the following ideas.

---

[6] From the lyrics of Bruce Springsteen's song *"Dancing in the Dark"*

PART FIVE – SMART MARKETING IDEAS

Idea #1 - Target Your Ideal Clients

Using your answers to questions 1 to 5 of your plan, create a list of clients you would like to work with based on specific criteria, such as industry, revenue, market share, whatever factors define your ideal client. Once you've established the criteria, create a list by searching the web and manually recording names and contact details or buy the list from an information provider such as **www.infousa.com**. There are a lot of other sites too, simply Google keywords like "Buy Sales Lists <Insert Your Local Area>" to find providers.

Make sure you have a systematic way to record and manage your leads. You can purchase Customer Relationship Management ("CRM") software or use an excel spreadsheet. It doesn't really matter what you use, as long as the system works for you.

Design a creative sales approach for contacting the people on your list. There are tonnes of ways to get your foot in the door, but the most effective method is to take decisive action, then record your results and conversion rate. If you're not getting results, take a step back, analyze what's going wrong and change your approach. Go after your ideal clients with non-stop persistence until you get a definite yes or no answer. Silence is not an answer.

Idea #2 - Network

Networking and word of mouth can be one of the most powerful marketing tactics for local business owners. I'm sure that no one can sell your services or products better than you. So create as many opportunities as you can to personally connect with potential customers.

[handwritten margin note: Chamber?]

Immediately when we think of networking we imagine big events with strangers we don't know. But networking isn't just that, it is any interaction with any person you meet, on any day, doing anything in your normal daily life. As mentioned earlier, you are your brand, every single second of every single day. Therefore, if you follow that logic, any person you meet at any second of any single day, is a potential customer.

So when people ask me "How do you start a conversation at a networking event?" the answer is: the same way you start any conversation with a person. Smile, say hello, and ask them a question about themselves. Show genuine interest in the person and enjoy the conversation.

Don't go to networking events with the singular objective of quickly and efficiently identifying potential customers and closing deals. The problem with that strategy is you're not connecting with people, you're assessing them. Nobody likes to be assessed or put into boxes based on whether you think they can be of benefit to you. That approach also discounts the potential connections a person may have that could help you. One thing is for sure, if someone doesn't like you, they will not do business with you and will not recommend you to anyone, regardless of how amazing your widgets are.

A person is much more than a product of what they do. They have social networks and if they like you, they will refer you to people that may want your services, even if they don't. When we connect with people we like, we have a natural tendency to want to help. So your singular objective at any event or meeting should be to <u>connect, not assess.</u>

Besides all that, life is short. Have fun doing your thing and you'll be amazed what opportunities come your way. Always be connecting - ABC!

Networking Tips

At networking events, there will be strangers you end up in a conversation with and you just can't find that connection. As in any part of your life, there will be people that you don't hit it off with, or you simply want to continue mingling without being rude. Here are three tips on how to move on without running to the bathroom or sculling back your drink so you have an excuse to leave.

1. The person you're talking to is at the networking event for the same reason you are: to meet people and mingle. Be honest about that and simply say, *"I'm really enjoying chatting with you but I'd like to keep mingling, would you like to come with me?"*

2. Offer to introduce them to someone else you know in the room. You can segue the introduction by saying you need to go but let me introduce you to X first or make the introduction and continue in the conversation.

3. If you really want to move on from the person to someone else simply say, *"Well, Jim, it was so nice to meet you and I wish you all the best with XYZ."* If you haven't already exchanged business cards, offer the person your card as a gesture to show that you really are glad you met them.

The third exit strategy is more difficult for most people to execute because it requires confidence and honesty in dealing with people. But I guarantee, if you try this, you'll be surprised at how liberating it feels to be honest with a person instead of making weak excuses to slink away. The key to this exit is to be sincere and honor the person. Make them feel that it really was your pleasure to meet them. If you're the person that always uses excuses to break from a conversation, I challenge you to try this at least once.

At the end of the day, you're at a networking event to meet people, don't get stuck with one person in a strained conversation because you're too scared to end it and approach another stranger. Be confident and push yourself beyond your comfort zone, that's what being an entrepreneur is about. That's how you'll grow and succeed at an exponential rate.

Follow Up

The first key to following up with connections from a networking event is to jot down a few notes on the person's business card to remind you who they are and what you discussed. Do this during the event (in private) or immediately afterwards while it's still fresh in your mind.

When you follow up, make sure you remind them who you are and include a little personal note about something you discussed to jog their memory of you. If they are a person you want to meet or call, make sure you give them a reason to continue the conversation and start building a relationship with you.

However you choose to follow up, DO NOT add the person's contact details to your e-mail subscriber database unless they specifically asked you to add them. It's rude and will not serve to build the relationship. A person must opt-in to your e-mail list to be considered a subscriber. Connecting at networking events is not about collecting business cards so you can increase your e-mail list. It's about creating relationships.

If you're not sure how the relationship can be continued after the event, add yourself to their social media networks and promote what they have to offer with comments, shares, likes etc. If they like your stuff, it's likely they will return the favor for you. You've now just created a social advocate for your brand, rather than a reluctant email subscriber who will likely unsubscribe or send your e-mails to spam for dishonoring your connection.

Remember, relationships are about giving, not just receiving.

PART FIVE – SMART MARKETING IDEAS

Idea #3 - Get Creative With Business Cards

The most effective business cards I've ever used were lip balms with my business logo and contact information custom printed on them. When people receive a business card they stash it away and rarely look at it again. A lip balm is used religiously and every use is a reminder to call you.

How can you be more creative with your business cards?

Idea #4 - Speak At Events

Very few people enjoy public speaking, but it is the most powerful way to present your message to a large group of people in a short amount of time and build your business. If this is a marketing strategy you're resisting due to fear or anxiety, sign up for a public speaking course, join a Toastmasters International group or consider improvisation classes to overcome your concerns. At some point in your life you'll likely be called upon to speak in front of a crowd, so take action now to alleviate your fears and build your confidence. Investing in your personal growth is always money well spent.

Some people may think it's a lot of work to speak at events, so here's a strategy to help break down the process.

- Create one presentation that really promotes your message and demonstrates to your ideal audience how you can solve their problem.

- Practice your presentation like crazy until you've truly mastered it.

- Write a one-page speaker sheet for your presentation including a short bio and make sure you use a professional headshot photo.

- Search online for venue calendars to identify organizations that are hosting events that will attract your ideal audience. Go to the organization's website and find out when they are taking submissions for speaker applications and either submit your application right then or set a reminder in your calendar.

- Add the event to your marketing plan and budget.

Whenever you present at speaking events make sure you maximize your profit potential by having something available for sale at the back of the room. Alternatively, provide free gifts or a competition with the goal of collecting contact information from your audience. However, some organizers will not allow you to do this, so make sure you're clear on the terms before you present at the event. If you're prohibited from selling, ask if they can provide video or images of you speaking that you can use in your products or on your website and other promotional materials.

Note that a key theme of this book is that your marketing strategies should continuously leverage your content creation efforts and focus on how to keep adding value for your customers. When you create an offer, ask yourself, how will I next connect with my customer? What else can I offer?

Idea #5 - Host Events

Clients love attending live events and the energy and buzz created gives you an opportunity to showcase true value for your clients, attract new clients and boost sales revenue. Events enable you to connect on a deeper level with clients and really find out what they want, need and expect. It's an effective way to check that you're still hitting the mark. A great idea is to host an annual event with promotional offers that aren't available at any other time to make the event really special.

Sure-fire tips for hosting a great event:

- Select a date, time and location that will suit your target audience.

- Send out invitations and advertise the event well in advance (provide at least 3-4 weeks notice).

- Make sure the invitation hypes up the event and give guests lots of reasons to attend. Some sort of "bring-a-friend" referral deal or promotion is also a good idea to boost numbers and attract new clients.

- Include an RSVP date. This will help you to organize and plan for catering and promotional gifts, gives the event credibility and reduces your anxiety regarding attendance levels.

- Send out media invitations and give journalists a reason to attend your event and/or write your own press releases.

- Call everyone on the guest list approx. 1-2 days before the event as a courtesy reminder and to confirm their attendance.

- Create a fun and energetic atmosphere at your event with music, lighting, decorations and entertainment.

- Schedule enough staff to work the event in order to maximize sales and make guests feel comfortable. Station an employee at the entrance and in key locations throughout the venue to help guide guests through the event and to provide a reliable point of contact if they need anything.

- Hand out flyers or use another method to visually advertise promotional offers that are only available at the event.

- Keep promotions simple and easy to understand, make it a no brainer for customers to buy. The electric atmosphere created at your event will make people feel good so they'll be more likely to spend money with you. However, if the promotions are confusing or require a lot of explanation, they'll feel like they need to think about it more and be less likely to buy.

- Thank guests as they are leaving the event and send out a thank-you note the next day.

- Post an article with photos about the event on your website, newsletter and social media platforms. This will help to attract more people next year.

While the event is still fresh in your memory, write down what worked and what didn't and assess the return on your investment. If the event was a success, add it to your marketing plan and budget for the following year. If it wasn't successful, write down how it can be improved for next time or why you won't include it in future plans.

Idea #6 - Write Guest Posts

Writing guest posts for other people's blogs is a great way to increase traffic to your website. Along with building web traffic it also demonstrates your expertise, builds credibility and helps customers find you. Regardless of whether you have a blog yourself, I would encourage you to write articles and blog posts for publications. If you find writing difficult, download dictation software and dictate your article content. Then hire a writer to finesse your work.

In line with this concept, the following ideas are offline marketing strategies for tapping other people's audiences and driving customers to your door.

Idea #7 - Create Strategic Partnerships

In my experience, partnerships are the most powerful and effective way to rapidly grow a business.

Identify complementary businesses in your area to partner with on cross-promotional campaigns. Schedule a meeting with the decision maker and arrive prepared with a list of things you can offer and would like to receive. Be professional and have a defined outcome for the meeting that you would like to achieve. Don't dismiss any potential partner until you've asked. Remember, the worst that can happen is they'll say, "No thank you, it's not right for us".

For example, when I owned a spa, one of the best partnerships we created was with a local gym. We enhanced their membership by having two staff members stand at the exit of the gym handing out free gift bags of spa goodies. The bags also contained a limited time special promotional offer and to ensure all members had an opportunity to take advantage of the deal, we posted flyers in the gym washrooms too.

When we initially met with the gym owner to discuss a cross-promotional partnership, we had expected they would want a lot from us in return, such as running promotions in our spa or placing a lead generation ballot box in our reception area. However, we were pleasantly surprised that the gym owner loved that we came into the gym every few weeks and gave out free goodies that were appropriate for his members. In his mind, that trade alone was a win-win situation.

We also created relationships with other businesses in our local area too. Take a walk around and write a list of complementary businesses in your area. What cross-promotional ideas could you pitch to them?

Online Partners

You may also find online partnerships too. For example, WaySpa is an online business that sells spa gift certificates that customers can use at any participating spa. WaySpa provides a free micro-site to promote your business on their website and charges a percentage of the face value of each gift certificate redeemed in your store. At one point, WaySpa gift certificates contributed up to 15% of our revenue and the marketing didn't cost us anything until a customer walked through the door. That's a great marketing partnership with a clear return on investment.

Can you partner with any online businesses in your industry?

Idea #8 - Attend Charity Events

One of the easiest ways to gain business exposure through other people's audiences is to participate in and donate to fundraising events in return for publicity. If you have a business that's constantly targeted by fundraisers requesting donations, view it as a great opportunity, not harassment.

As a spa owner, I received at least 6 donation requests every month. Although they were all very worthy causes (according to their pitch) there's no way we could agree to every request. Before donating to charities, make sure you have an annual budget (including the cost of donations such as products and gift certificates, not just money) and create a criteria checklist to guide your selection process.

Here's a sample guideline for assessing requests:

1. Is the event in line with your company's core values? This should be the first question you ask before agreeing to associate your business with another organization. One poor choice of association can have an ongoing detrimental effect on your reputation. It takes a lifetime to build trust and only a moment to destroy it.

2. Will the event attract attendees that live within the

local area? No matter how great your business is; people generally value convenience of location to their home or work when it comes to frequenting a store. If attendees do not live in the local area, is there another compelling reason to be involved?

3. How many and what sort of people will be attending? The answer to this question should also determine the value and type of donation you provide as well as guide your decision of whether to donate or not.

4. What type of publicity will the event generate? Sometimes the answer to this question isn't always clear at the outset. I recently read a story on facebook about an overweight dog that was nursed back to health by a foster carer. This dog was so fat he couldn't use his legs; he had to be carried around. The story included photos of the dogs' weight-loss progress and a "thank you" to the pet food company that donated his food and the centre that donated his swimming lessons! These companies donated because they believed in the cause, they couldn't have known the dog's story would go viral on facebook. What's my point? Publicity shouldn't be your only deciding factor. Always stay true to your company's core values.

5. Can you attend the event for free? As discussed earlier, networking and making connections is a

great promotional strategy for your business and demonstrates your genuine support for the charity. Attend the event; network; snap some photos for your website, newsletter and social media updates. Take a look around and ask yourself, was this a good use of my resources? Will I do this again? If the answer is yes, add the event to your marketing plan and budget for next year.

Regardless of your decision, make sure you reply to every request. It's a good business habit to acknowledge every person that contacts you. Create template responses so it doesn't take any time at all to be polite and professional.

PART FIVE – SMART MARKETING IDEAS

Idea #9 - Rent Your Space

If you have a venue that you could potentially rent out, do it. While you may not want to do this often, it's a great way to give your revenue a little boost on days when your store is generally quiet or closed.

The first step to attracting event hosts is to advertise somewhere on your website or in your store that the space is available for rent. If you have a space that really lends itself to being used as an event venue, such as an art gallery, consider adding your business to free online venue listings.

There are a few things to keep in mind when renting out your space.

1. Always have a signed contract in place that specifies the pricing and what's included and excluded. Be sure to specify the event start and end times and the cost that will be charged if the organizer exceeds the time allocation.

2. Always take a damage deposit.

3. Always take a non-refundable deposit on signing of the contract and collect the remaining amount prior to the event date.

4. Always have at least one of your employees or yourself at the event to make sure everything runs smoothly. When determining the amount of rent to charge, include the cost of your time in the calculation.

5. In line with the previous section on associating yourself with charities, make sure you know what the event is about and what is being promoted and that it fits with the core values of your business.

If an event organizer or partner approaches you with an offer that doesn't quite line up for you, don't jump to "no" straight away, think creatively. Always ask yourself, "Can I counter-offer to make this work? Here's an example of what I mean.

A Canadian magazine editor approached us to provide our spa as the venue for a beauty product promotional event being hosted for their readers. In return for using our space, we would receive free publicity in the national magazine plus the event would attract a large number of attendees that may become new customers.

Sounds great, right? But here was the dilemma.

The product being promoted was not organic and we would need to remove all of our product lines from the shelves. We only used and promoted organic beauty products, that was our primary core value. But this was a huge promotional opportunity and a chance to create a relationship with a national magazine publisher.

So what did we do? We counter-offered.

We explained that being associated with a non-organic beauty product could damage our business reputation; therefore we were willing to rent our venue to them and requested that our company name be excluded from any event advertising. In that counter-offer, we told them exactly how much the rent would be and what that included, such as the number and type of staff we would provide and the number of hours they could use the venue. They accepted.

Idea #10 - Be Newsworthy & Create A Media Kit

When starting your business create a media kit and send out press releases announcing your business launch. After the launch, business owners often ask me how to continue being newsworthy and generating media attention. Here's the two keys; 1) You must have a strong positioning statement that differentiates you in the marketplace; and 2) you need to do something, anything, that goes above and beyond your usual daily business activities. It doesn't need to be spectacular; it just needs to be more than what you do on an everyday basis. Then write your own press release and distribute it online through free press release sites.

You'll also want to start building out your media kit from day 1 so you're prepared with information that can be used to respond to interview requests. With every interview that you do, write down the questions that were asked and your responses and keep them in one well-structured document. Then, any time you receive a media request, you can respond quickly.

Hire a photographer and videographer to take high-resolution images and footage of your business that you can submit to editors along with your interview response. Remember that you are in control of the content that you distribute for your business. What you can't control is the conversation that stems from that content.

Being able to respond quickly and professionally to a media request shows that you're a business pro. Most media requests are fairly urgent and reporters like to work with businesses that can respond quickly. As you build media relationships, you'll soon start receiving unsolicited requests and you won't need to work as hard to get publicity.

Depending on your type of business, you may want to create a media kit section on your website where your logo and photos can be downloaded. This reduces the risk of poor quality web images being used and is worthwhile if you want people to promote your business without necessarily needing to contact you.

Idea #11 - Be "The Best" In Your City

This is one of the best-kept little marketing secrets that can sky rocket your business revenue and it's really simple.

In the first year of operation, for both my local Toronto businesses, I had them voted onto "Best of Toronto" and "Best in Canada" lists in popular online magazines. I'm sure you can imagine how great this publicity is for business, but here are the definitive advantages:

- Being voted onto a list is really exciting because everyone loves to win stuff and it will make you feel great about your business.

- That excitement creates buzz through your social media and email networks when the publication goes live. It also gives you something positive and different to talk about when promoting your business.

- The editors usually give you a variety of free and well-designed promotional material to use on your digital and print marketing material.

- This marketing material gives your business credibility and (in my opinion) is even better than customer testimonials because you've been awarded an honor by "impartial judges".

- All of this leads to increased brand awareness and sales revenue for your business.

But how do you become the "Best Of" something? Here's how in 3 easy steps:

1. Identify all of the publications with "Best Of" lists you'd like your business in. Online publications are the most beneficial as the article will live on the web for a long time giving you more return for your effort. You'll also be able to link to it in your marketing campaigns to create a viral effect on social media sites and to boost your search engine rankings.

2. Since most "Best Of" lists are issued annually, subscribe to the publications email list. Publishers will reach out to their community to ask readers to recommend nominees for the lists and to vote for the finalists. By subscribing to the publications email list you'll be notified of these requests.

3. When the list of nominees is distributed and voting begins, create an email and social media status updates to send out to your clients and friends asking them to vote for your business. Be sure to include:

- The website link for voting;

- Simple but specific steps on how to vote; and

- A clear reason why you are asking them to vote.

In my experience, 1 email broadcast only and a maximum of 2-3 well-crafted social media updates should be sufficient. While your subscribers obviously appreciate your business they will not appreciate multiple emails asking them to vote. So keep the email communication strictly limited to 1 broadcast and don't be pushy, a little humor will go a long way.

Idea #12 - Exhibit At Trade Shows

Trade shows can be categorized as buyer or browser shows depending on the theme. A show with buyers will generate a decent amount of sales on a promotion to make it a happy trip to the bank. A show with browsers will only be worthwhile if you create a promotion that enables you to track redemptions after the show.

While I am specifically discussing trade shows in this section, the real life experience I am about to share with you will demonstrate a universal fact. The environment will dictate a customer's emotional state and determine whether they will buy from you or not. Timing and location/platform of your offer is critical for maximizing sales. For example, if a person is researching on Google, it's likely they're just browsing. But if they're researching on Amazon, they're likely ready to buy.

Now, let me share with you my trade show experience to really hone this point.

When I owned a spa, we exhibited at two trade shows. One was a bridal show and one was a green living show. At the bridal show, most attendees arrived with specific information gathering goals in mind. They were browsing for deals on limos/cakes/venues etc. but they were not buying. Attendees of the bridal show were rushing through the exhibits, picking up information, throwing it in their bag and taking it home to sort through later. Really interested browsers would stop to talk in depth about services and appointments but these were few and most wanted to talk things over with "my fiancé/bridesmaids/mother" etc. before deciding.

On the other hand, the green living show was a lifestyle show filled with buyers. People at this show lined up at booths for deals and information. They were ready to buy on the spot, but more importantly, they were looking for organic beauty services and products that could be a permanent part of their lifestyle. This was a show where we found loyal customers, not one-time browsers. See the difference?

And to solidify this point, at the bridal show we took home approximately $1,500 in sales for the weekend and very few leads converted to sales. At the green living show we banked over $16,000 in 2 days! The exhibitor costs for both shows were about the same (including staffing & promo material), but the green living show brought more sales during the event and continued to generate more sales in the months to follow. Now, that is a decent return on investment.

If you're reading this and thinking, *"Yes, but I don't do trade shows for revenue, I do them to build my brand"*, you're lying to yourself. What you're really doing is throwing money at a marketing tactic and hoping it works. Please stop doing that. Don't pay any more money for any marketing until you know exactly how you will measure the return on your investment. And if you work with a marketing consultant, stop paying them until they can show you how they are tracking the return on your investment. If they can't, find someone who can.

Idea #13 - Create Promotional Offers

Love them or hate them, limited time only (urgency) and limited number only (scarcity) promotions work. Use them to create buzz, boost revenue and to reward your customers and attract new ones.

Many business owners believe a promotional offer always equates to a discount offer. However, if you're creative, promotions don't always need to involve offering discounts. Here's an example of a successful promotion we created for the spa without discounting.

We took a walk around the neighborhood and wrote a list of all the professional businesses in our area including 3 major banks, lawyers, doctors and dental offices. We thought about the needs of office workers and realized that, if we created an offer that enabled them to receive spa services during their lunch break with a time guarantee, that would be more enticing than a general discount offer. So we defined the idea and then called our bank manager and asked him what time the employees take their lunch breaks.

We printed rack cards with a lunchtime menu of services and included a guarantee that we could provide all services listed within a 30-50 minute timeframe. We included a description of each service that stated exactly what was included and we priced the services accordingly. The prices weren't discounted to entice clients to book; they were reduced to reflect that steps had been cut from the usual service to speed it up. The rack card also stated that the services were only available on weekdays from Monday to Friday between the hours of 12-2pm.

Now, distribution of the cards is important. We didn't just turn up and give them to a receptionist. We called and booked appointments to see the office manager of each business. We turned up looking professional, friendly and passionate about our business. Within an hour of returning from the final meeting, we had new clients calling to book appointments and one of the bank workers dropped in that evening to buy a very high valued spa package as a gift.

We saw an immediate return on our effort because we went out and connected with people instead of hoping people would find us.

A motivated business owner steps outside their store and makes things happen. What can you do to create opportunities for your business?

Idea #14 - Constantly Up-Sell

Upselling is when you persuade a customer to buy something in addition to or more expensive than the item they've decided to buy. McDonalds is the ultimate example of a company that trains its staff to up-sell on every purchase. For example, if you order a McDonalds burger, the cashier will ask if you'd like to "make it a combo". If you order a combo meal, the McDonalds cashier will ask if you'd like to "supersize" it (meaning to make it an extra large sized meal).

Make sure your staff can confidently up-sell a relevant product or service offering on every sale. It costs you money to attract clients to your business so the goal should be to sell as much as possible to every client who walks through your door and have them love you so they keep coming back for more. Clients appreciate knowledge and value; if your sales cycle focuses on this, clients will buy from you.

Take a good look at your sales cycle, are you leaving money on the table? Keep making offers to your customers until they say "no". The best time to make an offer is when they are already in the process of buying something or engaging in an experience with you. Always be ready to tell them what's next.

Idea #15 - Advertise

You'll notice that the strategies I've presented so far are virtually free to implement. There is so much you can do to create free or low cost marketing for your business that you don't really need to pay for advertising. However, if your budget enables you to pay for advertising, you should consider it.

As with every marketing strategy, you will need to ensure you're monitoring the return on investment. Although it's generally much easier because you know exactly how much you're spending, you do need to make sure you know exactly which advertising medium your customers are coming from.

If you're in start-up mode or on a tight budget, all of the tactics presented previously are much cheaper, and just as effective for a local business, as paid advertising, although, you may need to be a little more creative and tenacious.

Idea #16 - Loyalty and Referral Programs

One of my friends is seriously into martial arts. He used to go to a Muay Thai gym 3 times per week. He religiously purchased monthly passes at full price in advance. Then the gym started offering group buy deals and selling passes at 50% off to new customers only. Soon the gym was over capacity with new members trying out beginner classes. The equipment was being reserved for the larger beginner classes and instructors were spread thin trying to teach combined classes. When the gym increased their prices and had not extended any sort of promotion or thank you to loyal customers, my friend left and found himself a new gym.

Why am I telling you this? To illustrate one of the biggest mistakes business owners make; focusing all of their marketing efforts on attracting new customers and minimal effort on retaining existing customers. Or worse, they create a loyalty program but keep changing the rules and making it harder for customers to obtain the rewards because they miscalculated how much it would cost as the business grows.

It's important to offer your brand advocates something special. Reward them for helping you grow your business and thank them sincerely, because without them, you would not have a business. If you offer an ongoing loyalty program, like reward points, make sure you know your numbers before you launch the program. Constantly changing the rules and making it more difficult to obtain rewards will lose you points with your best customers. If you're just starting your business and don't know what the financials look like yet, avoid offering ongoing programs until your business is a little more mature.

Also, don't underestimate the power of a personal thank you. Rewarding customers doesn't always mean offering discounts and promotions, sometimes it's as simple as picking up the phone or hand writing a note and saying, "Thank you, I hope you enjoyed your experience with us".

Key Takeaways

✓ There are a tonne of different ways to market your business. You just need to get a little creative and focus.

✓ When launching a marketing campaign, consider the emotional state of consumers, on the platform you are using. Are they buying or browsing? Then ask yourself the following questions:

- For this campaign, what action do I want the customer to take?

- Are they in the right emotional state to take this action at the time I am asking?

- What do I need to do to lead them to the action I would like them to take?

✓ Ensure your customer acquisition efforts are balanced with customer retention programs.

✓ Convert potential customers into loyal brand advocates by continuously building trust and adding value.

✓ Always Be Connecting (ABC). Marketing is as much about building strong relationships, as it is about selling.

- ✓ Every time you create an offer, work out what other complementary products, services or gifts you can add to that offer as an incentive or up-sell. Always be thinking about the next connection you can make with your customer that will add value and keep them wanting to be in your sales cycle.

- ✓ Leverage your creation efforts by continuously adding things that build on the last thing you did.

- ✓ Before you spend any money on a marketing campaign, make sure you know how you will assess the return on your investment. If the return meets or exceeds your expectations, repeat, if not, don't do it again.

- ✓ Effective marketing is an active process. Go out and show the world how passionate you are about your business and you'll create opportunities bigger than you ever imagined.

PART SIX – THE MARKETING HIERARCHY OF SUCCESS

"In order to achieve "flow", "magic", "the zone", we start by being common and ordinary and workmanlike."

- Steven Pressfield

— PART SIX – THE MARKETING HIERARCHY OF SUCCESS —

How to Market Your Business Like A Pro

As a consultant I spend most of my life writing and speaking about business with entrepreneurs. I love receiving questions and comments from readers of my work and I take the time to respond to everything personally and in detail wherever I can.

But there's one common question (or variations of it) that tends to solicit a facetious response from me and that's *"What's the quickest way to make my business successful?"*

That question is like asking me *"How long is the piece of string I'm holding that you can't see?"*

The fact is, it doesn't really matter how I answer either of those questions because, without any information, my response can only be a stab in the dark that may or may not be helpful.

So from now on, when I receive questions like this, I'll be directing the inquirer to this section of the book where I'm about to expose my secret strategy for marketing your business like a pro.

The first thing you need to know is: **Pros don't take short cuts!**

Growing a successful business is like losing weight; it's a daily, focused process consisting of testing and tweaking ideas and monitoring results. You don't go for one run and suddenly have the body of a pro athlete. You set goals and each day you do a little bit of the right stuff that moves you closer to achieving them. Then when you reach those goals you set new goals and you start working towards those. Over time it becomes a healthy obsession that's just part of what you do all the time.

The "Marketing Hierarchy of Success" that I'm about to share with you is loosely based on Abraham Maslow's concept of the human hierarchy of needs.

Maslow studied people who he described as "exemplary" such as Abraham Lincoln and Eleanor Roosevelt, to devise a 5-tier hierarchy that describes the development of healthy individuals. The broad concept is that people are first motivated to fulfill their basic physiological needs (food, water, air etc.) before advancing and mastering each of the upper levels.

At the highest level a person achieves self-actualization where they are capable of continuously growing and realizing their full potential. Maslow suggests that a person's lower level needs must be met in order to avoid unpleasant feelings such as anxiety. As the person advances upwards, their needs stem from a

PART SIX – THE MARKETING HIERARCHY OF SUCCESS

desire to grow rather than to avoid pain.

So how does this relate to business marketing and how can you use it?

Below I'll share with you the details of my 3-tier "Marketing Hierarchy of Success". At the lowest level, business owners are performing the basic marketing tactics required to keep their business humming along. When they can consistently perform the basics at tier one and add tier two activities to their marketing they start to experience rapid business growth. Adding tier 3 activities into the mix is about reaching a level of marketing mastery. At the highest level, the business owner has built a system of defined processes while continuously learning and incorporating new marketing ideas. They are constantly monitoring, reviewing and redefining their marketing plan and strategy.

As with Maslow's theory, the "Marketing Hierarchy of Success" is based on the expectation that the entrepreneur masters each level before advancing and incorporating the next level.

Let's discuss in detail the three marketing tiers that drive business success.

Tier 1: Surviving

A business owner that's operating at a tier one level is maintaining their business by consistently performing the daily, weekly and monthly marketing activities required to keep things going.

These include, but are not defined or limited to, the following types of activities:

- Interacting with and having daily conversations with customers
- Sending email broadcasts
- Writing social media posts
- Building website traffic
- Pre-booking appointments
- Offering promotions and specials

Tier one activities are performed consistently and frequently. They are the basic marketing activities required to attract and retain customers. At the lowest level of performance they enable an owner to keep the lights on while juggling monthly cash flow. At the highest level of performance, tier one activities result in the slow and steady growth of the company.

PART SIX – THE MARKETING HIERARCHY OF SUCCESS

Tier 2: Thriving

Tier two is where all the fun starts to happen and things get really exciting! This is when events like a media promotion, speaking event, tradeshow or anniversary party occur. The result is a massive revenue spike for a day or two then small incremental gains continue for months or years afterward as the point-in-time effort continues to payoff.

Tier two activities are not ad-hoc events that happen by accident. They are planned at the beginning of every year and can be relied upon to boost revenue.

At this level, the business owner is performing tier one and two activities using defined processes and tools. Their annual marketing plan and budget includes itemized tier one and two activities that they know, with reasonable certainty, will result in a minimum of X dollars for the year. The processes include constant monitoring and review of results and refining future marketing plans to effectively utilize all available resources. This is a healthy place to be on the road to business success.

Tier 3: Optimizing

Pros know that they must continuously learn and try new techniques and strategies that keep them sharp and at the top of their game. When a business owner reaches tier three, they are continuously learning, innovating, checking results and tweaking things to make it work or dropping it because it doesn't work.

Tier three activities are ad-hoc and untested new ideas. They are the cream on top of your marketing pie. They are expected, in the sense that a "miscellaneous" bucket was included in the annual marketing budget and plan. However, the exact activity and complete details may not be known until later in the year.

When the results of a tier three activity are positive and repeatable, it is moved down the hierarchy and reclassified as a tier one or two activity next year. It is removed from the "miscellaneous" bucket and itemized in the marketing plan and budget of the following year. Planning includes lessons learned and details of any changes or improvements needed to accelerate the results of activities in future years. Questions 11-15 of your Smart Marketing Plan provide a guide for assessing results and planning future marketing campaigns.

The diagram below provides an overview of the "Marketing Hierarchy of Success".

PART SIX – THE MARKETING HIERARCHY OF SUCCESS

The Marketing Hierarchy of Success

Tier 3: Optimizing
- New, ad-hoc ideas
- Planned for in "Miscellaneous" budget
- Learn, try & test results
- Repeat or trash

Tier 2: Thriving
- Consistent & Planned
- Quarterly or annual
- Repeatable activities
- Causes large revenue spikes & incremental gains overtime

Tier 1: Surviving
- Consistent & Planned
- Daily, weekly, monthly
- Repeatable activities
- Basic requirement to be successful

Trash or Repeat?

New Ideas

Planned Repeatable Activities

Media promotions, guest articles, tradeshows, promotions with partners, anniversary party, speaking/hosting events etc.

Daily conversations with customers, email opt-ins & broadcasts, pre-booking appointments, promotional offers, social media posts, increasing website traffic, soliciting customer reviews & feedback etc.

Copyright. All Rights Reserved. www.trudymurphy.com

In 1943, Maslow coined the term "meta-motivation" meaning the motivation of people who go beyond the scope of their basic needs and strive for constant betterment to reach their full potential. These days we call this "hustle".

If you want to build a successful business you need a whole lot of hustle!

Using the "Marketing Hierarchy of Success" to market your business like a pro will definitely take a lot of hustle because it requires you to master and perform on all three levels. Unfortunately, many business owners are inconsistent and oscillate between each level but are never able to perform at all three levels simultaneously.

When you can build a marketing system of defined processes and activities, your business will reach it's full potential.

PART SEVEN – ACTION CREATES INSPIRATION

"Write down every possible action you could take to start making money immediately. Do whatever actions jump out at you. Don't over think this. Just do it. Life is short."

- Frank Kern

5 Tips For Being A Kick Butt Marketer!

I know that some of you reading this, despite everything I've just shared with you, will still be thinking something along these lines:

"This is great Trudy, but I'm hopeless at marketing, I'll never be good at it"; or

"This all makes sense, but I'm terrible at selling" or my favorite …

"I just don't know what to say to close deals; I need a salesperson to do it for me".

If you associate any sort of negative connotation with yourself when selling your services or products, or you generally feel nervous when selling, you're not thinking about it in the right terms.

Here are my top 5 tips to help you get over self-doubt and be a kick butt marketer.

1. Selling is simply talking to someone about something you know.

For example, in writing this book, I'm talking to you about local business marketing. It's a topic that I know. In doing so, I hope that a percentage of you will like what I have to say and buy some of my other products or services. But some of you won't and that's ok too. Because, my focus is on sharing my knowledge with you and adding value to your life and business venture. If all I do is strive to achieve that one goal, everything else will take care of itself. When you consistently add value, people will want to work with you, they will want to buy from you, but most importantly, they will become loyal customers if you keep taking care of them. It's not "selling", it's "knowledge sharing".

2. K.I.S.S. (Keep It Simple Stupid).

The most effective marketing involves very clear and simple wording, offerings and descriptions. When we overcomplicate things by pairing too many offerings together or being overly clever with wording, the customer ends up confused and won't act or buy in this emotional state. Be clear, concise and simple with wording and don't provide too many options simultaneously.

PART SEVEN – ACTION CREATES INSPIRATION

3. Focus on benefits, not features.

When marketing your product or service always answer the customer's "What's in it for me?" question by focusing on the benefits, not the features. Features describe what a product does and how it works. Features don't tell a customer what's in for them.

Examples of product benefits include: save time, save money, feel sexier, impress your friends etc. Benefits tap into a customer's emotional state and make buying your product a "no brainer". Since marketing is essentially about motivating another person to take a specific action, you need to think like your customers and answer their questions and potential objections upfront.

4. Close the Deal.

The golden rule of closing a deal is to present the pricing and then shut up. Don't soften it by suggesting pricing can be discounted or try to justify it; you should have already demonstrated the value proposition during your pitch. Give the client a chance to respond before you say anything else. If you don't, they'll know immediately that you are not confident in the price you've presented and that you lack negotiating skills. In which case, you'll never be paid the price you ask.

5. Don't Give Up!

If you're not getting the results you were hoping for, try a different approach. No one gets everything right the first time. And as an entrepreneur, you're going to encounter obstacles all the time. In fact, you should just expect them.

The way to succeed is to take a step back, evaluate the situation and then change your approach. Keep tweaking things until it works. Better yet, seek out a mentor who's done it before and ask for help. Don't waste your energy trying to figure things out alone if someone else can get you there faster with less stress.

Bonus Tip: Online Reviews & Testimonials Sell

According to a 2014 study[7], 88% of North American consumers surveyed said they trust online reviews of a business as much as a personal recommendation by a friend. That trust is higher if there are multiple reviews to read that reinforce each other and show a consistent story. This statistic demonstrates the importance of following up with your customers after the sale to check their results and to encourage them to provide a review or testimonial. The more positive feedback you can point to about your business, the easier it will become for you to attract and sell to new customers.

---

[7] *"Local Consumer Review Survey 2014"* by Bright Local

PART SEVEN – ACTION CREATES INSPIRATION

Finalize Your Smart Marketing Plan & Execute

Once you've finalized parts 1-10 of your Smart Marketing Plan, print it out and place it somewhere you can easily see it every day. A plan is a living, breathing document that should be referred to frequently to guide your daily "To Do" lists and keep you on track towards achieving your goals. You've put in the effort to create your plan, now it's time to execute.

As you complete each of your marketing campaigns, be sure to record the results against questions 11-15. The answers to this section will help to build your plan for next year.

I hope this book has fuelled a passion in you to actively market your business. I hope you've come up with your own creative ideas and that you've written them into your marketing plan as you read the book.

If you haven't had a chance to grab your free bonus offers yet, be sure to do that now at:

www.smartmarketingforlocalbusinesses.com/the-plan

Key Takeaways

- ✓ If there's one thing I'd like you to know after reading this book, it's that success is not born from luck. Being an entrepreneur can feel lonely, but if you take focused action every day to grow your business, doors will open and create a natural momentum and inspiration that keeps you moving forward.

- ✓ Be persistent and never give up your big audacious dreams!

COMMIT TO YOUR GOALS

If this book has inspired you to implement a new marketing strategy or be more active and passionate about your business, are you willing to commit and announce your intentions?

Connect with me and tell me your plans. I'd love to hear from you and help you achieve your goals. Be bold. Act now.

www.trudymurphy.com/contact

You've dreamed of it, now be brave and live it.

Wishing you every success in business and life.

- Trudy

ABOUT THE AUTHOR

Trudy Murphy is a corporate consultant turned serial entrepreneur. Today, Trudy leverages her years of corporate experience in process design and change management to bring big business ideas to local business owners. Having successfully owned and sold local businesses herself, she is acutely aware of the challenges facing entrepreneurs.

Trudy speaks and writes about business leadership and marketing for entrepreneurs and executives. You can find her at:

www.trudymurphy.com

SMART MARKETING FOR LOCAL BUSINESSES

Made in the USA
San Bernardino, CA
30 April 2018